Copyright © 2023 by Tamika Hill

Nothing contained in this book should be construed as legal advice.

Printed in the United States of America

Diversity Amplified:

A DEIB Strategy Planner

"The strength of an organization lies in its diverse perspectives."

-THILL

Diversity Amplified: A DEIB Strategy Planner

Imagine a workplace where everyone, regardless of background or identity, feels included and valued in the organization. That's the power of DEIB: diversity, equity, inclusion, and belonging.

But what exactly does DEIB mean in the workplace?

<u>Diversity</u> refers to employing and encouraging people of different races, backgrounds, beliefs, and behaviors within an organization.

<u>Equity</u> provides every employee the resources and opportunities to achieve an equal outcome.

<u>Inclusion</u> refers to an organization's ability to value, respect, and support its employees, regardless of their background.

<u>Belonging</u> is an employee's perception of acceptance and understanding they've received within the workplace.

For several years, companies emphasized the importance of DEIB in their planning. However, organizations have begun to recognize the value of adding belonging to their DEIB strategies.

DEIB is becoming increasingly important in today's world as many organizations strive to create an inclusive and diverse workforce. With globalization and the increasing number of people from different backgrounds working together, organizations need to recognize the importance of diversity. DEIB planning helps companies understand the diversity of their workforce and develop policies that support an inclusive work environment.

Belonging is a critical aspect of DEIB planning. Employees need to feel that their opinions are heard and that they are part of a team. So, by promoting a culture of belonging, organizations can ensure that every employee feels valued and included, especially those who previously felt like they didn't belong.

Every human being has an innate need to feel accepted within social groups; this includes family, friend groups, and especially at work. Employees who feel a sense of belonging are more likely to be happy and productive in the workplace. On the other hand, those who don't feel that sense of belonging are more likely to become burnt out, unproductive, and uninterested in the company's goals.

Organizations thrive by utilizing their employees' diverse perspectives, experiences, and talents. Yet, despite the benefits of embracing diversity, many organizations find themselves at a crossroads, unsure of how to navigate toward a truly inclusive workplace.

To develop a comprehensive and effective DEIB strategy, organizations need to follow the following steps:

1. **Shift the Culture:** Transform your organization's culture from reactive to proactive by creating a shared vision that informs and aligns employees with the company's mission. An organization can effectively foster a proactive culture by involving key stakeholders and communicating this vision.

2. **Share the Commitment:** Get everyone in the organization on board by making DEIB a top priority across all levels of the company. Continued efforts, training, and consistent support are required to ensure the changes implemented are successful.

3. **Promote Respect and Open-mindedness:** A respectful and inclusive workplace environment requires deliberate planning, but cultivating fairness, encouraging freedom of expression, and authenticity fosters a culture that values diverse perspectives and innovation.

4. **Embed DEIB in Operations:** Integrate DEIB into every facet of the organization. Revise existing systems from recruitment to performance management to establish a lasting system that prioritizes DEI.

5. **Measure Outcomes for Alignment:** Collect and analyze data on DEIB efforts to gain insight that can align metrics with goals.

Without the right guidance and strategies in place, companies often miss the mark in their efforts to create a comprehensive DEIB strategy. This is where the DEIB strategy planner comes into play.

This planner will provide you with the goal-setting tools required to achieve your long and short-term goals. You'll be guided through three activities that will provide you with insight into the existing organizational culture regarding DEIB. These insights will aid in setting the following goals:

- Long-term Goals: The goals that will take a year or more to accomplish.
- Mid-Year Goals: The goals that will take six months to accomplish.
- Quarterly Goals: The goals that will take ninety days to accomplish.
- Monthly Goals: The goals that will take thirty days to accomplish.
- Weekly Goals: The goals that you will set out to accomplish every week.

Be strategic when setting goals. Being overly ambitious with the implementation of a new strategy can result in confusion and fatigue among staff, hindering the organization's ability to progress. Conversely, if a laid-back approach is adopted and DEIB efforts aren't enforced by management, the organization will fail to emphasize the importance of inclusivity.

Some goals that you might consider as part of your DEIB strategy include:

- Increase spending to diverse suppliers by 25% in one year.
- Introduce diversity training for all employees within the first six months.
- Audit HR policies to eliminate biases within the first three months.

Regardless of what your goals may be when planning, remember that they should be achievable and measurable.

To aid in assessing the impact of DEIB initiatives, this planner also includes an evaluation section that's divided into four quarters. Each quarter includes a 30-day, 60-day, and 90-day evaluation sheet with questions to assist in reviewing the organization's progress.

In the following section, we'll explore the tools for setting and measuring the impact of DEIB strategies.

DEIB Goal Setting Tools

Establishing a solid foundation for a comprehensive Diversity, Equity, Inclusion, and Belonging (DEIB) strategy entails creating a roadmap for both short and long-term goals that align with the organization's overarching vision. These objectives should be transformative, drive long-lasting change, and embody the essence of DEIB and a sense of belonging within the organization.

When establishing goals for DEIB, consider the following prompts and activities to guide your planning:

Assessing Current Status:

Conduct a comprehensive review of current DEIB initiatives within the organization.

How would you describe the existing organizational culture regarding DEIB?

____

____

____

____

____

What practices or policies already support DEIB efforts, and where are the areas for improvement?

____

____

____

____

____

Diversity Amplified: A DEIB Strategy Planner

<u>Stakeholder Engagement and Input:</u>

Provide anonymous suggestion boxes or digital surveys for employees and leadership to share ideas or concerns regarding DEIB.

What do the employees and leadership perceive as the organization's stance on diversity, equity, inclusion, and belonging?

____

____

____

____

What are the primary hurdles impeding DEIB progress within the organization?

____

____

____

____

____

____

Diversity Amplified: A DEIB Strategy Planner

<u>Aligning Objectives with Vision:</u>

Conduct brainstorming sessions with cross-functional teams to outline achievable DEIB goals over the course of one year.

How do the proposed objectives align with the organization's overarching long-term vision for DEIB?

____

____

____

____

What steps can be practically implemented to move closer to the organization's desired DEIB outcomes?

____

____

____

____

____

Diversity Amplified: A DEIB Strategy Planner

Which specific aspects of DEIB should be the primary focus to create meaningful change in the next year?

____

____

____

____

What resources, whether financial, human, or technological, will be essential to achieve these goals?

____

____

____

____

How can leadership and stakeholders provide support or allocate resources to ensure success? goal attainment?

____

____

____

____

"Inclusion isn't just a goal; it's the heartbeat of a thriving, equitable workplace."

-THILL

Now that you have a comprehensive idea of your organization's culture regarding DEIB, it's time to set your long and short-term goals:

What are your Long-term Goals?

____

____

____

____

____

____

What are your Mid-Year Goals?

____

____

____

____

____

____

Diversity Amplified: A DEIB Strategy Planner

What are your Quarterly Goals?

Q1: ____

Q2: ____

Q3: ____

Q4: ____

What are your Monthly Goals?

Month 1: ____

Month 2: ____

Month 3: ____

Month 4: ____

Month 5: ____

Month 6: ____

Month 7: ____

Month 8: ____

Month 9: ____

Month 10: ____

Month 11: ____

Month 12: ____

Diversity Amplified: A DEIB Strategy Planner

What are your Weekly Goals?

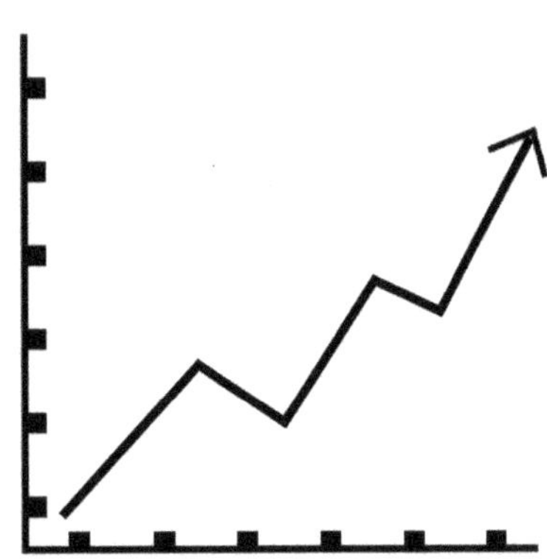

"Within every goal achieved is the story of an organization's persistence."
-THILL

First Quarter Evaluation

<u>Q1 30-Day Evaluation</u>

Congratulations on completing the first 30 days of the first quarter. Before you continue with implementing your DEIB strategic plan, take this opportunity to pause and evaluate your organization's progress so far.

What progress has been achieved within these past 30 days of implementing the DEIB strategies?

____

____

____

____

____

Are the outlined steps and initial goals on track with the planned timeline? If no, what strategies moved you toward your goal and which did not?

____

____

____

____

____

Diversity Amplified: A DEIB Strategy Planner

How have employees responded to the ongoing DEIB strategies?

____

____

____

____

Did any unexpected challenges arise during the initial phase of implementation? How were they addressed?

____

____

____

____

____

"*Equity is a non-negotiable foundation for a just society.*"

-THILL

<u>Q1 60-Day Evaluation</u>

Congratulations on completing the first 60 days of the first quarter. Before you continue with implementing your DEIB strategic plan, take this opportunity to pause and evaluate your organization's progress so far.

Are there any notable improvements observed compared to this quarter's initial 30 days?

____

____

____

____

____

____

How effectively have the organization's actions aligned with the overall goals set for this quarter?

____

____

____

____

____

____

Are there any changes in employee feedback compared to this quarter's initial stages?

____

____

____

____

Have there been any significant adaptations in the strategies employed based on feedback received within the previous 30 days?

____

____

____

____

____

"Every milestone reached is a testament to an organization's commitment to its vision."

-THILL

Q1 90-Day Evaluation

Congratulations on completing the entire first quarter. Before you continue with implementing your DEIB strategic plan, take this opportunity to pause and evaluate your organization's progress so far.

Have the organization's initiatives increased, decreased, or sustained momentum throughout this quarter?

____

____

____

____

____

____

What observable impact or changes have been witnessed in the workplace culture or environment due to DEIB efforts?

____

____

____

____

____

How adaptable have the implemented strategies been in response to the evolving needs of the workplace?

____

____

____

____

____

What additional support or involvement from leadership could further strengthen these efforts?

____

____

____

____

____

"Inclusivity isn't a checkbox; it's a commitment to honoring every voice and perspective."

-THILL

Second Quarter Evaluation

<u>Q2 30-Day Evaluation</u>

Congratulations on completing the first 30 days of the second quarter. Before you continue with implementing your DEIB strategic plan, take this opportunity to pause and evaluate your organization's progress so far.

What progress has been achieved within these past 30 days of implementing the DEIB strategies?

____

____

____

____

____

Are the outlined steps and initial goals on track with the planned timeline? If no, what strategies moved you toward your goal and which did not?

____

____

____

____

____

How have employees responded to the ongoing DEIB strategies?

____

____

____

____

Did any unexpected challenges arise during the initial phase of implementation? How were they addressed?

____

____

____

____

____

"A clear vision is the foundation upon which an organization builds its legacy."
-THILL

<u>Q2 60-Day Evaluation</u>

Congratulations on completing the first 60 days of the second quarter. Before you continue with implementing your DEIB strategic plan, take this opportunity to pause and evaluate your organization's progress so far.

Are there any notable improvements observed compared to this quarter's initial 30 days?

____

____

____

____

____

____

How effectively have the organization's actions aligned with the overall goals set for this quarter?

____

____

____

____

____

____

Are there any changes in employee feedback compared to this quarter's initial stages?

____

____

____

____

Have there been any significant adaptations in the strategies employed based on feedback received within the previous 30 days?

____

____

____

____

"Leadership means not only having a vision but ensuring that vision includes everyone."

-THILL

Diversity Amplified: A DEIB Strategy Planner

<u>Q2 90-Day Evaluation</u>

Congratulations on completing the entire second quarter. Before you continue with implementing your DEIB strategic plan, take this opportunity to pause and evaluate your organization's progress so far.

Have the organization's initiatives increased, decreased, or sustained momentum throughout this quarter?

____

____

____

____

____

What observable impact or changes have been witnessed in the workplace culture or environment due to DEIB efforts?

____

____

____

____

____

How adaptable have the implemented strategies been in response to the evolving needs of the workplace?

____

____

____

____

____

What additional support or involvement from leadership could further strengthen these efforts?

____

____

____

____

____

"Diversity opens the door; equity ensures everyone can walk through it."

-THILL

Third Quarter Evaluation

<u>Q3 30-Day Evaluation</u>

Congratulations on completing the first 30 days of the third quarter. Before you continue with implementing your DEIB strategic plan, take this opportunity to pause and evaluate your organization's progress so far.

What progress has been achieved within these past 30 days of implementing the DEIB strategies?

____

____

____

____

Are the outlined steps and initial goals on track with the planned timeline? If no, what strategies moved you toward your goal and which did not?

____

____

____

____

____

How have employees responded to the ongoing DEIB strategies?

____

____

____

____

Did any unexpected challenges arise during the initial phase of implementation? How were they addressed?

____

____

____

____

"Equity is more than a goal, it's a guide through every decision towards fairness."

-THILL

Diversity Amplified: A DEIB Strategy Planner

<u>Q3 60-Day Evaluation</u>

Congratulations on completing the first 60 days of the third quarter. Before you continue with implementing your DEIB strategic plan, take this opportunity to pause and evaluate your organization's progress so far.

Are there any notable improvements observed compared to this quarter's initial 30 days?

____

____

____

____

____

How effectively have the organization's actions aligned with the overall goals set for this quarter?

____

____

____

____

____

Are there any changes in employee feedback compared to this quarter's initial stages?

____

____

____

____

Have there been any significant adaptations in the strategies employed based on feedback received within the previous 30 days?

____

____

____

____

"True leadership advocates for diversity not as an obligation but as an opportunity."

-THILL

<u>Q3 90-Day Evaluation</u>

Congratulations on completing the entire third quarter. Before you continue with implementing your DEIB strategic plan, take this opportunity to pause and evaluate your organization's progress so far.

Have the organization's initiatives increased, decreased, or sustained momentum throughout this quarter?

____

____

____

____

____

What observable impact or changes have been witnessed in the workplace culture or environment due to DEIB efforts?

____

____

____

____

____

How adaptable have the implemented strategies been in response to the evolving needs of the workplace?

____

____

____

____

____

What additional support or involvement from leadership could further strengthen these efforts?

____

____

____

____

____

"Inclusion isn't about fitting in; it's about belonging and feeling valued."

-THILL

Fourth Quarter Evaluation

<u>Q4 30-Day Evaluation</u>

Congratulations on completing the first 30 days of the fourth quarter. Before you continue with implementing your DEIB strategic plan, take this opportunity to pause and evaluate your organization's progress so far.

What progress has been achieved within these past 30 days of implementing the DEIB strategies?

____

____

____

____

Are the outlined steps and initial goals on track with the planned timeline? If no, what strategies moved you toward your goal and which did not?

____

____

____

____

____

Diversity Amplified: A DEIB Strategy Planner

How have employees responded to the ongoing DEIB strategies?

____

____

____

____

Did any unexpected challenges arise during the initial phase of implementation? How were they addressed?

____

____

____

____

"Setting goals is the first step; achieving them is the leap toward excellence."
-THILL

Diversity Amplified: A DEIB Strategy Planner

<u>Q4 60-Day Evaluation</u>

Congratulations on completing the first 60 days of the fourth quarter. Before you continue with implementing your DEIB strategic plan, take this opportunity to pause and evaluate your organization's progress so far.

Are there any notable improvements observed compared to this quarter's initial 30 days?

____

____

____

____

____

How effectively have the organization's actions aligned with the overall goals set for this quarter?

____

____

____

____

____

____

Are there any changes in employee feedback compared to this quarter's initial stages?

____

____

____

____

Have there been any significant adaptations in the strategies employed based on feedback received within the previous 30 days?

____

____

____

____

"Belonging is not just about fitting in, it's about being valued for who you are and what you bring to the table."

-THILL

<u>Q4 90-Day Evaluation</u>

Congratulations on completing an entire year of DEIB efforts within your organization. Let's take a moment to evaluate the implementation of your DEIB strategic plan and assess your organization's progress throughout this year.

What valuable lessons or insights have emerged from the year-long DEIB journey? How can these lessons shape future DEIB strategies or ongoing organizational efforts?

____

____

____

____

____

____

____

____

____

____

____

Diversity Amplified: A DEIB Strategy Planner

What major milestones and objectives have been successfully achieved by the end of the year?

____

____

____

____

____

How can the organization leverage its DEIB successes to continue fostering an inclusive workplace culture?

____

____

____

____

____

Congratulations on your remarkable dedication to fostering a workplace where diversity, equity, inclusion, and belonging are the foundation of your organization.

As you celebrate the milestones achieved, remember that this is just the beginning. Continue celebrating diversity, embracing equity, and nurturing an inclusive workplace within your organization.

Your commitment to continuous improvement ensures a future where everyone feels respected, heard, and empowered within your workplace and our society.
-THILL